Gerrit Rietveld

Rietveld Schröder House

Residential Masterpieces 32
Gerrit Rietveld
Rietveld Schröder House

Text by Ida van Zijl
Photographed and edited by Yoshio Futagawa
Art direction: Gan Hosoya

Printed and bound in Japan

ISBN 978-4-87140-565-2 C1352

Gerrit Rietveld

Rietveld Schröder House

Utrecht, The Netherlands, 1923-24

Text by Ida van Zijl

Photographed by Yoshio Futagawa

世界現代住宅全集32

ヘリット・リートフェルト
リートフェルト・シュレーダー邸
オランダ, ユトレヒト　1923‑24

文：イダ・ファン・ゼイル

企画：二川幸夫

撮影・編集：二川由夫

リートフェルト・シュレーダー邸 ── イダ・ファン・ゼイル
The Rietveld Schröder House *by Ida van Zijl*

〈背景〉

2000年，「リートフェルト・シュレーダー邸」は，二つの基準によってユネスコの世界遺産に登録された。一つは，ユトレヒトにあるこの住宅が，近代建築運動の象徴であり，デ・ステイルによって導かれた純粋なアイディアと思想の創造的で卓越した表現であること。もう一つは，デザインと空間の使い方における先鋭的なアプローチにより，「シュレーダー邸」が近代建築の発展において重要な位置を占めている点である。[1]

　ヘリット・リートフェルトは，クライアントのトゥルース・シュレーダー・シュレッダーと共に1924年にこの住宅を完成させた。それが彼の最初の建築作品であると同時に，その後の作品の方向性を決める鍵となった。この住宅の建築家，クライアント，そして設計プロセスについて私たちは何を知っているだろうか。

ヘリット・トーマス・リートフェルト（1888-1964年）は，家具屋をを営む職人の次男として，ユトレヒトに生まれた。彼は小学校を終えた11歳から父親のもとで働き，優れた職人になるための実践的な訓練やスキルを身につける傍ら，ユトレヒト芸術工芸博物館，芸術産業教育会の夜間授業にも通った。また，ユトレヒトの建築家P・J・C・クラールハマーの夜間講座にも数年間通い，当時の先端的な建築の動向を学んだ。彼は宝石商C・J・A・ベヘールに雇われていた時期もあり，そこでヤン・W・アイセリホやエーリヒ・ウィフマンなどの革新的なデザイナーと出会った。

　1917年，リートフェルトはアドリアーン・ファン・オステードラーンに家具工房を開いた。ここで彼は最初の実験的な椅子をデザインし，それがオランダの前衛運動であるデ・ステイルのメンバーであった建築家ロバート・ファント・ホッフの目

に留まり，グループに招かれた。その後1919年には，彼のデザインした家具が雑誌『デ・ステイル』の第9号に子供用の椅子，第11号の第2巻に無塗装のスラットチェアが掲載された。これ以来，リートフェルトの名は近代運動と切り離せないものとなったのである。彼はオランダおよび国際的な前衛芸術に対する知識を深め，テオ・ファン・ドゥースブルフ，J・J・P・アウトらによるいくつかのプロジェクトに参加した。

　しかし，これは彼に重要な仕事をもたらすものではなかった。1924年まで，彼は主に家具職人として働き，いくつかの店舗と室内の改装を手がけた。彼の飛躍の機会はまったく別の方向から訪れたのである。

トゥルース・シュレッダーは裕福なカトリックの中産階級出身で，1889年にダヴェンターに生まれた。22歳のとき，彼女はユトレヒトの弁護士，フリッツ・シュレーダーと結婚した。トゥルース・シュレーダー・シュレッダーは，勉強をすることを望み，子供はつくらないことを結婚前に取り決めていたが，夫は思っていたよりも保守的であった。のちに3人の子供をもうけたが，関係はますます破綻していき，彼女にとってこの不幸な結婚は重荷となっていった。大邸宅での生活をより快適にするために，彼女と夫は彼女の好みに合わせた部屋を用意することに決めた。そこで，フリッツ・シュレーダーの顧客であるアムステルダムのガウト＆ツィルヴェルスミット商会の店舗の改修を任されていたリートフェルトに白羽の矢が立った。

　リートフェルトとトゥルースが初めて会ったのは1911年，彼が父親とともに彼女の夫へ大きな机を届けた時だった。86歳当時のトゥルース・シュレーダーによる

Background

In 2000 the *Rietveld Schröder House* was placed on the UNESCO World Heritage List. The decision was based on two criteria. First: *The Rietveld Schröderhuis* in Utrecht is an icon of the Modern Movement in architecture and an outstanding expression of human creative genius in its purity of ideas and concepts as developed by the De Stijl movement; and second: With its radical approach to design and the use of space, *the Rietveld Schröderhuis* occupies a seminal position in the development of architecture in the modern age.[1]

Gerrit Rietveld built the house in 1924 together with his client Truus Schröder-Schräder. It was his first architectural creation and would prove to be the key work for his entire oeuvre. What do we know about the architect, the client and the design process?

Gerrit Thomas Rietveld (1888-1964) was born in Utrecht as the second son of a cabinet maker who had his own business. After elementary school, at the age of 11, he went to work with his father. Besides completing the practical training and developing the skills necessary to become a good craftsman, he took evening classes at the art and industry educational society of the Utrecht Museum of Arts and Crafts. For several years he also attended evening courses with the Utrecht architect, P. J. C. Klaarhamer, where he learned about the latest developments in architecture. He was employed by the jeweler, C. J. A. Begeer, for a time, where he met innovative designers like Jan W. Eisenlöffel and Erich Wichman.

In 1917 he opened his own furniture workshop in the Adriaan van Ostadelaan in Utrecht. It was here that he produced his first experimental chair designs, which attracted the attention of the architect Robert van't Hoff, a member of the Dutch avant-garde movement De Stijl. He

invited Rietveld to join the group and shortly after two of Rietvelds design were published in the magazine De Stijl: a children's chair in the no. 9 issue and the unpainted slat chair in the no. 11 issue of volume 2, 1919. From that moment on Rietveld was inextricably linked with the modern movement. He became acquainted with the Dutch and international avant-garde and was involved in several projects with, among others, Theo van Doesburg and J. J. P. Oud.

However, this did not bring him commissions of any significance. Up to 1924, he worked mainly as a cabinet maker, although he also completed some interiors and shop alterations. The breakthrough in his development came from a completely different direction.

Truus Schräder, who was born in Deventer in 1889, came from a wealthy catholic middle-class background. At the age of 22 she married the Utrecht lawyer, Frits Schröder. Truus Schröder-Schräder wanted to study as had been agreed before her marriage, and not have any children, but her husband turned out to be more conservative than she had hoped. They had three children but drifted apart more and more. For Truus Schröder this unhappy marriage was an emotional burden. To make her life more comfortable in their big mansion, she and her husband decided she should have a room of her own, arranged to her taste. Rietveld, who had done the remodeling of the shop of the Goud & Zilversmid Compagnie in Amsterdam,a client of Frits Schröder, got the commission.

Rietveld and Truus met for the first time in 1911 when he and his father delivered a huge desk for her husband. According to the 86-year-old Truus Schröder, there was already at that time a click between the young fiancée and the son of the cabinet maker. They both loathed the old-fashioned style of the desk. During the following years Rietveld

と，その時すでに若い婚約者と家具職人の息子は意気投合していた。彼らは共に古風なデザインの机を嫌っていた。その後の数年間，リートフェルトは小さな修理のために時々家を訪れ，トゥルースの部屋を改修した後は，数人の同僚を連れて自分の仕事を見に来たりもした。トゥルース・シュレーダーは，子供たちに配慮してか，生涯を通じて彼らの恋愛の始まりについて口にせず，当初から「ソウルメイト」であったとを強調した。1974年になって初めて，オランダの週刊誌のインタヴューで，彼女は二人が恋愛関係にあったことを認めたが，彼女の要望に反して，記者が誌面に「恋愛関係」という言葉を使ったことに失望した。トゥルース・シュレーダーは，「シュレーダー邸」の設計過程において，常に濃密なコラボレーションを求めていた。彼女は自分が単にクライアントと見なされることを嫌い，リートフェルトの最初のデザインを一目見てどのように却下したのか，そして，眺望，光，平面計画を出発点に，どう設計を再スタートさせたかを説明した。デザインにおける彼女の役割を尋ねられると，彼女はいつも家を子供に例えた。「子供が母親の何を受け継ぎ，また父親の何を引き継いだかはわかりませんよね」[2]。

1923年10月3日に夫が亡くなった後，彼女は以前より小さく実用的な住宅が必要となったに違いない。窮屈だった結婚生活から解放され，彼女は住まいと幼い3人の子供たちとの生活を自分らしい方法で整えたいと決意していた。当初，彼女とリートフェルトは改修可能な中古住宅を探していたが，予想以上に難航した。そこで彼女はリートフェルトの意見に従い，家を建てる決心をした。偶然にも二人は，家を建てるのに最もふさわしい場所として，ユトレヒト郊外の同じ敷地を選んだのだった。数年後，リートフェルトは述べている。「……あの椅子（レッドアンドブルー・チェアー，1919年）と同じ原理に基づいて住宅をつくる機会を得たとき，私はその好機を逃さなかった」[3]。こうした背景のなか，ヘリット・リートフェルトとトゥルース・シュレーダーの協働が実現した。

〈設計のプロセスと建物の来歴〉
建築家としてのリートフェルトの仕事の方法は，家具職人としての修練の影響を受けている。彼は縮尺模型と原寸のプロトタイプによってアイディアを展開するのが常だった。我々が知る限り，「シュレーダー邸」の設計プロセスにおいてつくられたのは，3枚のスケッチと二つの模型のみで，模型の一つは厚紙とガラス，マッチ棒でつくられており，その後失われたままである。

1階平面と壁の描かれた初期案からは，1階の平面構成がみてとれるだけである。ホールから南東側の広い客間と北東隅の台所へと分かれ，台所はベッドのある個室へと続いている。メモによると，ガラスで拡張された居間を，一部屋根が高い2階に置くよう計画されていたことがわかる。おそらくこのデザインは，トゥルース・シュレーダーが一目で却下した。「とても素敵な小さな家でしたが，私好みではありませんでした。実際は私が思っていたよりも魅力的だったと思いますが……私は明らかに全く違う何かを期待していたのです」[4]。ここからリートフェルトとトゥルース・シュレーダーの協働が始まった。最終的な配置と平面構成は，二人の熱心な議論の中から生まれたのだった。2階のレイアウトは見事である。階段の吹抜けの隣にはストーブと煙突があり，それを中心に可動式の間仕切りで複数の部屋に分割できる一つのオープンスペースとなっている。1階は，当時の建築基準にあわせて，ホールと四つの部屋，キッチン，トイレを備えた一

Design Process and Building History
sometimes came to the house for small repairs and after the alteration of Truus' room he brought several colleagues to see his work. For all of her life, Truus Schröder was vague about the beginnings of their love affair, perhaps for the sake of the children, clouding the circumstances and emphasizing they were 'soulmates' from the beginning. It was only in 1974 that she admitted in an interview in a Dutch weekly that they had had a love affair, being disappointed that, against her wishes, the journalist used the words "love affair" in the final text. Intense collaboration during the design process of the Schröder House was something Truus Schröder always stipulated. She hated to be considered just a client, explaining how she dismissed Rietvelds' first design after giving it only a superficial glance. And how they began anew, taking the view, the light, and the ground plan as starting points. When asked what exactly her part was in the design, she always compared the house with a child: "Then you don't really know what it has inherited from the mother and what from the father."[2]

What is certain is that after her husband's death on 3 October 1923, Truus Schröder wanted a smaller and more practical house. Moreover, she was determined to arrange her home and her life with three small children in a way that suited her better than the stifling environment of her marriage. At first she and Rietveld looked for an existing house that could be remodeled. This proved more difficult than expected. At Rietveld's suggestion, she decided to have a house built. Independently they chose the same plot of land at the outskirts of the city as the most suitable building site. Years later Rietveld commented: "... when I got the chance to make a house based the same principles as that chair [the Red Blue Chair], I seized it eagerly."[3] Against this background the collaboration between Gerrit Rietveld and Truus Schröder took place.

Design Process and Building History
The way Rietveld worked as an architect was influenced by his training as a cabinet maker. He was used to developing his ideas through small-scale models and full-size prototypes. As far as we know, only three sketches and two models were made during the design process. One of the models, made from cardboard, glass and matchsticks, has since been lost.

In a preliminary drawing showing the ground-plan and the walls, only the layout of the ground floor is shown: a hall leads to a large sitting room on the south-east side and to the kitchen, which is situated at the north-east corner of the house. The kitchen leads into a bed-sitting room. According to a note on the drawing, a living room with a glazed extension was planned for the upper floor under a partly raised roof. Probably this is the design that Truus Schröder rejected at first sight. "It was a very nice little house, but it wasn't my kind of thing at all. In fact I think it was more attractive than I realized ... I clearly must have had something completely different in mind."[4] Rietveld started again, this time together with Truus Schröder. The final layout and ground plan of the two floors came about during the course of their intense discussions. The layout of the upper floor is spectacular: it is one open space that can be divided into several rooms by sliding partitions, with the stove and chimney in the center next to the stairwell where you enter the room. The ground floor has a more conventional layout with a hall, four rooms, a kitchen and a toilet, to meet the building code of the time. Rietveld had to bring the two floors together visually: "It was very difficult to prevent that lower part from being too massive compared with the upper part, because then it would have been two things, different ideas. That is how it started out and then the concept gradually became clear. But initially it of course became a massive thing when seen from the outside, because it is incredibly difficult to shake off a

般的な配置である。リートフェルトは，上下階を視覚的に結びつける必要を感じ，次のように述べている。「1階のヴォリュームが2階に比べてどうしても大きくなりすぎる。それは，二つのもの——異なるアイディアからできているからである。そうやってスタートし，徐々にコンセプトが明確になってきたが，最初は外から見るとマッシブなものになってしまった。なぜならあるアイディアを打ち捨てて譲歩するのは非常に難しいからだ」。[5] 最初の模型である「マッシブなもの」は，おそらくそれほど世間を沸かせるものではなかった。この案は，どっしりとして窓や扉となる開口をもつ長方形の建物であった。2階の南東角の後退した窓と北西側のバルコニーだけが均一な壁面線を打ち破る。スカイライトはこのときすでに付いていた。窓枠の黒と玄関扉の黄色とともに描かれた灰色と白の壁面は，この住宅の空間構成とは何の関係も持っていないようなパターンを形づくっていた。二人ともこの模型に満足していなかったのかもしれない。いずれにせよ，リートフェルトは革新的なファサードをデザインし続けた。それは，パリのギャラリー・ローゼンバーグで開催されたデ・スティル展のために，コーネリアス・ファン・エーステレンとテオ・ファン・ドゥースブルフがデザインした「メゾン・パルティキュリエール」と「メゾン・ダルティスト」に触発されたのだろう。そして，1924年7月2日に建設許可がおりたのである。

　2枚の外観スケッチと建築許可の申請書に添付された図面は，細かいところが実施案と多少異なるだけである。主な違いは当時の建築制限により変更された箇所で，すべての部屋は1階にあり，2階のリビングエリアは，「屋根裏」と称して偽装された。スライド式の壁の可動域を示す，かすかな点線からこの階のレイアウトと用途がすでに決められていたことは明らかであった。

1924年6月18日の土地取得から8月中旬の着工までの約2ヶ月で，リートフェルトは23枚の実施図面を作成しただけだった。デザインの大部分は現場で検討され，リートフェルトの口頭での指示によってつくられた。1924年12月31日にトゥルース・シュレーダーがこの家に引っ越してきた時も，内壁の塗装にはまだ手がつけられておらず，家具の一部は未完成だった。トゥルース・シュレーダーがスイスで短い休暇を過ごしている間に，リートフェルトは2階の床の色彩計画を考案し，制作していた。このように猛烈な勢いで始まった後，工事はいくぶんペースを落とし最終段階へと進んでいった。この住宅の至る所に見られる考え抜かれた細部のデザインは，家具職人兼建築家の彼と，クライアント兼コラボレーターのトゥルースとの独特な関係性を背景にしてのみ理解し得るだろう。

トゥルース・シュレーダーは，モンテッソーリの小学校に貸していた短い期間を除き，この家で一生を過ごした。彼女の3人の子供が家を出た後，彼女は1階のいくつかの部屋を貸しに出した。リートフェルトがこの家に住むようになったのは，1957年に彼の妻が亡くなってからのことで，その後1964年に自身が亡くなるまで彼女と一緒に暮らした。そしてトゥルースは，彼の死後21年間近く生きた。60年の間，彼女は生活の変化にあわせて建物を改修してきたが，これらはリートフェルトの指示に全面的に従って行なわれた。1985年に彼女が亡くなった後，この住宅は1920年代のオリジナルの状態に修復され，ユトレヒト中央博物館の管理下に置かれ，以来，一般に公開されている。

specific idea, to let something go."[5] "The massive thing" is probably the first model which did not turn out to be all that sensational. The form of this house was massive: a rectangular block with openings for windows and doors. Only the recessed window section at the south-east corner of the upper floor and the balcony on the north-west side provided any break in the line of the wall. The skylight was already present. Gray and white surfaces formed with the black of the window frames and the yellow of the front door a pattern that appeared to have no relationship with the spatial arrangement of the house. Maybe they both were not really satisfied with this model. Rietveld, in any case, went on to design the revolutionary facades, perhaps inspired by the Maison Particulière and the Maison d'Artiste designed by Cornelis van Eesteren and Theo van Doesburg for the De Stijl exhibition the previous year in Galerie Rosenberg in Paris. On the 2 July, 1924, this design was submitted along with the application for a building permit.

　The two sketches of the exterior from that phase and the drawing sent in with the application for a building permit differ only in minor respects from the final result. The differences mainly reflect changes required by the building regulations of the day. All the rooms are on the ground floor, while the function of the upper floor as a living area is disguised by calling it an "attic". The faint dotted lines which show the extended positions of the sliding walls are evidence that the function and layout of this floor had already been determined.

About two months passed between the acquisition of the land on 18 June 1924 and the beginning of construction in mid-August. Rietveld made only 23 working drawings; much of the design was thought up on site and built to Rietveld's oral instructions. When Truus Schröder moved into the house on 31 December 1924, some of the furniture had not yet

been made and the interior still had to be painted. Rietveld devised and produced the color pattern for the upstairs floor while Truus Schröder was on a short holiday in Switzerland. After this feverish start, the house grew into its final shape at a somewhat slower pace. Much in the house, such as the painstaking detailing, can only be understood against the background of the unique relationship between this cabinet maker/architect and his client/collaborator.

Truus Schröder lived all her life in this house, except for a short period when she rented it to a Montessori elementary school. After her three children left the house, she rented some rooms on the ground floor. Rietveld came to live with her after his wife passed away in 1957 and stayed until his death in 1964. Truus survived him by almost 21 years. During these 60 years she adapted the house to accommodate the changes in her personal circumstances. These alterations were carried out entirely according to Rietveld's instructions. After her death in 1985, the house was restored to the original state of the 1920s and brought under the custody of the Centraal Museum. Since then it has been open to the public.

The Architectural Features of the House
The house is approximately 10 meters wide, 7.7 meters deep and 6 meters high, and consists of two floors. The front door, divided into an upper and lower part of the kind common in Dutch farmhouses, leads into a small hall with a toilet and a staircase with a landing. To the right of the hall is the living/kitchen area, behind which is a bed sitting room for the maid. Beneath this room is the cellar which can be reached via the stairs from the kitchen. Off the hall to the left is a small study. Directly opposite the front door is a studio space which Rietveld used as

Composition of
vertical and horizontal elements

〈建築的特徴〉

建物は間口約10メートル，奥行7.7メートル，高さ6メートルの2階建てである。オランダの農家によく見られる，上下に分かれた玄関扉を入ると，トイレがある小さなホールと踊り場付きの階段がある。ホールの右手は居間兼台所，その奥に使用人室がある。使用人室の下には地下食料庫があり，台所から階段を下りてアクセスする。ホール左手は小さな書斎，玄関の反対側にはリートフェルトが1933年まで仕事場として使用していたスタジオがある。このスタジオと使用人室との間にもうひとつ別の仕事部屋があり，物置や暗室として使われていた。2階へ続く階段は，踊り場の引戸の先にある。2階のスペースは完全に開放され，浴室と洗面所のみが固定された壁で囲まれており，階段室の隣には煙突がある。このオープン・スペースはスライド式の間仕切りにより居間，シュレーダー夫人の寝室，2人の娘のための部屋，息子のための部屋，そして踊り場に仕切ることができる。室内に設置されたスライド式の壁は，軽くて動かしやすいように，木枠とコルクシートでつくられている。階段は，リビングエリアとガラスの屋根から，木製のパーティション，合板パネル，スライド式のガラス・パネル，そして木製のハッチで仕切ることができる。階段室の周囲の手摺りに取り付けられた短い梯子を使って天窓内のハッチまで登り，そこから屋根にアクセスできる。屋根には北東の外壁につけられた鉄製の梯子からも上がることができる。

建設にあたり，リートフェルは工法と材料に関して伝統的なものと現代的なものの双方を組み合わせて用いた。建物はコンクリートの柱に梁を重ねて支持されている。レンガ積みの壁はI形鋼の梁で補強され，プラスターで仕上げられてい

る。床，屋根組，窓枠は木材でつくられ，I形鋼の梁で支持されたバルコニーのみコンクリートが使われている。屋根は陸屋根で，一般的なアスファルト防水が施されている。合理的な配慮から，全般に従来型の工法を用いている。リートフェルトは外壁にコンクリートを使いたかったが，当時，それはあまりに複雑で高価であった。実際，彼はデザインを実現するために，どのような材料や工法を用いるかについては，それほどこだわらなかった。

〈インテリア〉

ヘリット・リートフェルトとトゥルース・シュレーダーの選んだ敷地は街の外れにあった。敷地は地平線まで広がる牧草地に向かって傾斜している。この住宅は，プリンス・ヘンドリックラーン通りの終点に建つ隣家の開口部のない側壁を背に建てられた。トゥルース・シュレーダーはプライバシーを損なわず，自由な気分でいられ，広々とした景色を楽しめる2階に住みたいと考え，実用的な諸室は1階に配置された。これは伝統的な「1階と2階」という分け方ではあるが，当時としては非常に珍しい間取りであった。彼女は子供たちと近くで生活したいと考え，彼らの寝室を2階に置いたからである。

　螺旋階段から広い開放的なリビングエリアに足を踏み入れると，まず目に飛び込んでくるのは四方から差し込んでいる豊かな陽光である。窓から，バルコニーのガラス戸から，正面や側壁の開口部から，そして，階段室の上の天窓から陽の光が降り注いでいる。広く水平に広がるガラス窓の日よけとなる屋根の張り出しは，太陽高度が高い時の日射をやわらげる役目を果たしている。各壁面に一つずつ，計三つのバルコニーによって，室内から室外へスムーズに連続する。建築

---

a work room until 1933. Between this studio and the maid's room, there is another small working space used for storage and a dark room. The staircase leading to the upper floor is situated behind the sliding door on the landing. This space is completely open, except for the toilet. The chimney is located next to the stairwell. This open space can be divided by sliding partitions into a living area, a bedroom for Mrs. Schröder, a bed sitting room for her two daughters, a bed sitting room for her son, and a landing. The sliding walls in the interior, which had to be light and easy to handle, are made of cork sheets with wooden frames. The landing can be screened off from the living area and the glass structure on the roof by wooden partitions, plywood panels, sliding glass panels and a wooden hatch. Using a short ladder fitted to the balustrade around the stairwell, one can climb up to the hatch and gain access to the roof through a door in the skylight. Outside, the roof can also be reached from the north-east balcony via an iron ladder on the wall.

For the construction, Rietveld used a combination of traditional and modern techniques and materials. The house stands on concrete pillars and a layer of concrete beams. The brick walls are strengthened by iron I-beams and finished with plaster. Wood has been used for the floors, the roof structure and the window frames. Concrete was used only for the balconies, which are supported by iron I-beams. For the roof, asphalt, commonly used for flat roofs, was employed. The choice of this largely traditional method of building was dictated by practical considerations. Rietveld wanted concrete for the exterior walls, but this was too complicated and too expensive. In fact, he didn't mind so much about the materials or building techniques that were used as long as the visual and spatial aspects of his design were realized.

The Interior

The piece of land that Gerrit Rietveld and Truus Schröder had chosen was on the outskirts of the city. The site sloped down towards meadows that stretched out to the horizon. The house was built against the blank side wall of the last house in the Prins Hendriklaan. Truus Schröder wanted to live upstairs where she could feel free and enjoy the expansive view without losing her privacy. The more utilitarian rooms were located downstairs. In some way this resembled the traditional division into "upstairs and downstairs". But the house had a very unusual ground plan, because she wanted her children near her and had placed their sleeping spaces on the upper floor.

When you enter the large open space of the living area via the spiral staircase, the first thing that strikes you is the enormous amount of light that streams into the house on all sides: through windows and glass balcony doors in the front and side walls and through the glass skylight above the stairwell. The overhanging parts of the roofs, which function as awnings above the wide horizontal glass sections, temper the light when the sun is high in the sky. Three balconies, one on each wall, provide a smooth transition from the interior to the exterior. The absolute high point in this architectural approach is the placement of the two windows that abut perpendicularly to form the southeast corner. When these windows are open, there is no longer any corner and the parapet appears to be the balustrade of a partially enclosed balcony. This construct dissolves the boundary between interior and exterior.

Furthermore, Rietveld used the same materials for the interior and exterior walls: brick, wood and iron beams, and enhanced the unity between interior and exterior by color and finishing. He diminished the physical characteristics of the materials by painting everything white, gray, black, blue, yellow and red. The gray wall of the girls' room/sleep-

的アプローチの最大のポイントは，直角に接する南東隅の二つの窓である。これらの窓をあけると，隅が無くなり，腰壁はバルコニーを部分的に囲む手摺りのように見える。こうして，内部と外部との境界は消え去ってしまう。

　リートフェルトは内壁と外壁にレンガ，木，鉄骨梁など同じ素材を使い，色と仕上げによって内外の統一感を高めた。またすべてを白，灰色，黒，青，黄，赤に塗ることで，素材が本来持っている物質感を抑えた。娘たちの部屋のベッドが置かれた灰色の壁は，バルコニーの脇の壁まで伸びている。I形鋼の梁は内外ともむき出し。同色で塗られた木製の梁と共に，灰色，白，黒にペイントされた面に対して，線形要素として際立った対比をみせている。

　リートフェルトは，ベッド，食器棚，テーブル，椅子，その他，可動あるいはつくり付けの家具を，広いオープン・スペース内の構成要素として用いた。ここでもまた，各々の要素と素材は色彩を与えられることによって，建築的に統合される。床，天井，壁，家具は一体となって，立体的な色彩構成による空間の分節をつくりだしている。室内はいわば，快適な「家具の集合体」である。

　1階の各部屋は壁で分割されている。空間の連続性を生み出すために，台所とトイレへ続くドアの上とホールと書斎の間の壁の上には大型の照明がつけられた。薄青色のホールの天井が書斎の黒い天井に反射する。また，両端を木のブロックに挟まれた管状の蛍光灯で構成された天井照明が二つ設置され，二つの部屋の間に視覚的なつながりを生んでいる。仕切壁はI形に突き出ており，ホール側では大人用の背の高いコートラックと子供用の低いコートラックが設置され，書斎側には書棚と折畳みテーブルが置かれた。1階の機能的なレイアウトが，この住宅の建築形態を決定するのに役立ったことは明らかである。

　書斎は，リートフェルトが家具を使って空間を形づくるのに膨大な時間を費やしたことを示している。窓の近くには，4本脚の可動式のスツールと壁に固定された背もたれと肘掛からなる座席を設計した。この窓際の席に合わせて，折畳み式の小さな机がつくられた。ここからは，牧草地を見渡すことができる。1階の窓と2階のバルコニーの床の間には，外部に飛び出した収納スペースがある。このバルコニーの下に，青色に塗られた木製のベンチが，書斎の椅子と同じ高さにつくられた。ガラス戸を開くと，内と外の分け目はなくなり，内外の要素が隅々まで統合される。2階の東隅と同様，この住宅を実際に構成する面を遥かに越えて広がる空間を体験することになる。

〈外部〉

「シュレーダー邸」の外壁は，水平，垂直な面と，互いに垂直または平行な直線的な要素が，非対称形で三次元的に構成されている。これらの構成要素は，視覚的には独立している。リートフェルトはこうした効果を，面や線の接点を延ばすことによってつくりだした。南東正面のバルコニーの手摺壁は，窓の前にあたかも宙に浮かんでいるように見える。バルコニーを支持するI形鋼は，独立して立ち，バルコニーの水平面の上まで延びている。南西面と南東面が出会うところで，リートフェルトは，それぞれの独立性を強調するために，南西壁を高くして白に，南東壁を幅広で低くしダークグレーに塗装した。つまり，閉じた角部ではなく，無限の空間にある独立した二つの面が接しているということである。そして，ドアや窓のための開口がある巨大な壁ではなく，三次元の色の構成として設計されたファサードが現れる。リートフェルトは，「レッドアンドブルー・チェ

ing corner runs through into the side wall of the balcony. The iron I-beams have been left exposed on the inside and outside. Together with the wooden beams painted the same colors, they form a striking linear contrast with the gray, white and black surfaces.

Rietveld brought some structure into the large open space by the position of the beds, cupboards, tables, chairs and other movable and permanently fixed pieces of furniture. Here, too, an architectonic unity was achieved by having color dominate over the individual elements and materials. The floor, the ceiling, the walls and the furniture together provide the articulation of the space in a three-dimensional color composition. As a result, the interior is a "Gesamtmöbel" suitable for living.

On the ground floor, the rooms are separated by partitions. To create a sense of spatial continuity, large overhead lights have been positioned above the doors leading to the kitchen and toilet and the wall between the hall and the study. The lavender blue of the hall ceiling is reflected in the black ceiling of the study. Also, the two identical ceiling lamps, designed as tubular bulbs between wooden blocks, establish a visual connection between the two rooms. The dividing wall has an I-shaped projection. A tall coat rack for grown-ups and a lower one for children have been placed in the hall ; in the study this space is used for bookshelves and a folding table. It is clear that from the outset the functional layout of the ground floor helped to determine the architectural form of the house.

The study provides an example of the great lengths Rietveld went to in using furniture to shape space. Near the window, he designed a seating accommodation consisting of a movable stool with four legs along with a back and armrest fixed to the wall. A small folding table was made to go with the window seat. This seat offered a wide view over the meadows. Between the window and the floor of the balcony, there is

storage space which is actually outside the house under the balcony. Under the shelter of this balcony, a wood bench, painted blue, has been made of the same height as the chair in the study. When the glass door is open the distinction between inside and outside disappears as a result of the detailed articulation of the interior and exterior elements. Just as in the east corner on the first floor, we experience with our senses a spatial quality that extends beyond the physical limits material surface of the house.

The Exterior

The exterior walls of the Schröder House are asymmetrical, three-dimensional compositions, constructed from horizontal and vertical surfaces and a few linear elements that are perpendicular or parallel to each other. These structural components are visually independent. Rietveld achieved this effect by having a surface or line run past the point where the two touch. The vertical balcony wall on the south-east frontage appears to float in front of the window. The I-beams which support the balconies are freestanding and extend above the horizontal surface of the balconies. Where the walls of the south-west frontage and the south-east frontage meet, Rietveld emphasizes their independence by making the south-west wall a little higher and painted white, and the south-east a little wider, lower and painted dark grey. So, instead of an enclosed angle, there is a point of contact between two independent surfaces in an infinite space. And instead of massive walls with openings for doors and windows, we see facades designed as a three-dimensional color compositions. Rietveld had experimented with these principles of form and spatial arrangement in his earlier furniture designs, such as the Red Blue and the Berlin chair.

Color is an important instrument in this interplay of lines and sur-

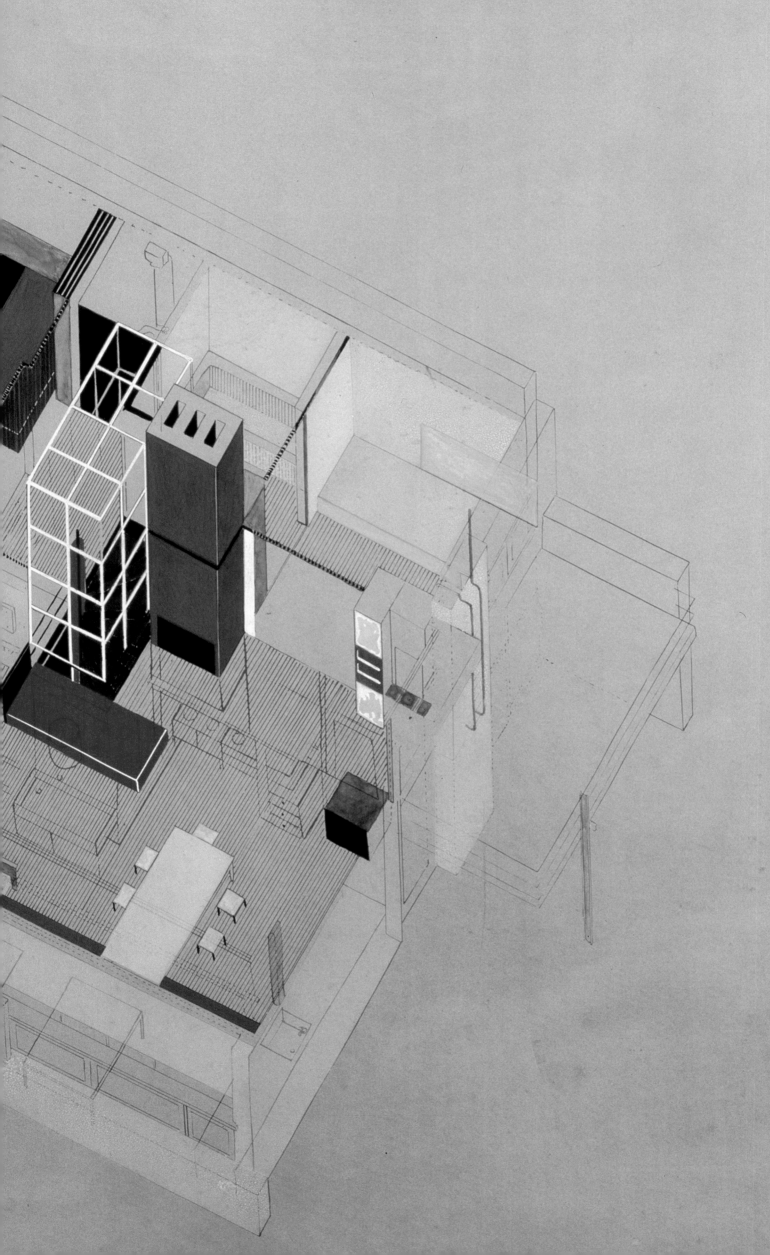

Axonometric

ア」や「ベルリン・チェア」などの初期の家具デザインに，こうした形と空間配列の原理を実験的に取り入れていた。

このような線と面との相互作用にとって，色彩は重要な道具であった。白，黒，さまざまな階調の灰色が，光の反射の強さに影響を与え，空間の中での面の位置が決められた。この色は面を後退させて見せることになるだろうか，それとも前進させるのだろうか。赤，黄，青がこの立体的な構成にアクセントを与えた。リートフェルトのデザインは，静的なものではない。オランダ特有の刻々と変化する光によって，白い帯のように放射される陽光から，暗い灰色の雨の空まで，一日の時間帯や季節によっても変わる。スライド式のパネルや白いカーテン，濃紺のシャッターを閉めると，オープンスペースを小さな居心地の良い部屋に分割できる。この住宅は，リートフェルトの，「……住宅は単なる生活の背景である」[6]という要求を満たす。

〈「シュレーダー邸」に住む〉
これらの形式性は，純粋に美的な要求に支配されているわけではない。建築の新しい潮流と同じくらい，生活に対する視点が「シュレーダー邸」の最終案に影響を与えている。「シュレーダー邸」は，個性と社会性，そして落ち着きと快適さの調和を探し求めたものである。オープン・プランの平面構成は，壁によっていくつかに分割できる。分割された各スペースには，水道，ガスが引かれ，戸口が付いている。快適さは家具，備品によってではなく，セントラル・ヒーティング，食洗機，レコードプレーヤー付きの棚といった当時では並外れて贅沢な設備を備えることによって生まれている。

1963年，リートフェルトはこう書いている。「人間が猛獣と本質的に同じ性質をもっているという矛盾を，なぜ表立って認めるべきではないのだろうか。木は水と空気のみを必要とし，環境と調和して無防備に立ち，それでいて木陰と果実を与えてくれる。私たちはそんな樹木の力強さを持ち合わせない。私たちもそうできたらと思う。……建築の歴史を振り返ると，人間の自己過信と権力の象徴として優れた形の建築物があるが，むしろ空間をもっと大切にしようではないか。そのために，私たちは可能な限り冷静に，空間の境界線を構築していこう。私たちの生活の喜びや豊かさは，住宅における中流階級的な完成度や設備の完璧さに左右されるのではなく，本質的な欲求と結びついた空間の質という合理的な方法から得ようではないか。抑制することは貧しいことではない。反対にそれは真実を体験するための唯一かつ最も人間的な方法なのである。私たちのもつ知覚能力の本質は，簡潔さのもつ豊かさを共に経験するための方法を示しているのだ」。[7]

〈リートフェルトの作品における「シュレーダー邸」の位置〉
リートフェルトの「シュレーダー邸」は，デ・ステイルの建築的記念碑として歴史に名を刻んできた。これはある程度正当なことであるといえよう。1924年，テオ・ファン・ドゥースブルフによって出版された宣言は，「シュレーダー邸」のための論理的な青写真とも読める。[8]同時に，ここから「三次元のモンドリアン」という言葉が使われた場合，この住宅に対する，一方的で間違った見方につながることになる。正確には，色彩の使い方において，リートフェルトの進め方は異なっているし，ファン・ドゥースブルフやピート・モンドリアンとは正反対でさえあるのだ。

faces. White, black and different shades of gray are used to influence the intensity of the reflection of light that in turn determines the position of the surface in space: is it receding or does it seem to come forward? Red, yellow and blue provide accentuation in these three-dimensional compositions. Rietveld's design is anything but static. Due to the ever-changing daylight in Holland, changing from snatches of bright sunlight to dark rainy skies, the sense of space is quite different at different times of the day and in the different seasons. Besides that, by closing the sliding panels, the white curtains or dark-blue shutters, the open space can be divided into small cozy rooms, fulfilling Rietveld's requirement that: "… a house is just a background for living."[6]

Living in Rietveld's Schröder House
These formal qualities are not dictated by purely aesthetic principles. The design of the Schröder House is rooted in a view of life that had at least as much influence on the final design as the new trends in architecture. The Schröder House represents a search for a harmony between individuality and sense of community, between sobriety and comfort. The open floor plan can be divided up by walls into separate spaces, each of which has its own running water, gas and exit to the outside. Comfort has not been sought in soft furnishings, but in central heating, a dishwasher and a cupboard with a record player which in those days represented an exceptional degree of luxury.

In 1963 Rietveld wrote: "Why shouldn't the conflict that we have essentially the same nature as the beasts of prey be openly recognized; we do not have the strength of a tree, which only needs some water and air, and stands unprotected in harmony with its environment and still provides shade and fruits; if only we could achieve that. … The whole of

architectural history shows us fine forms of built masses-monuments to man's self-assurance and might. Let us rather put the emphasis on space and be as sober as possible in the construction of its boundaries. Let our joy of living and wealth not be dependent on the middle-class completeness of our dwellings and the perfection of the installations, but on the appreciation of the economic way the quality of space ties in with these essential needs. Constraint is not impoverishment, on the contrary it is the only and most human way of experiencing reality. … the nature of our powers of perception shows us the way to experience together the affluence of austerity."[7]

The Place of the Schröder House in Rietveld's Work
Rietveld's Schröder House has entered history as the architectural monument of De Stijl. To some degree, this is justified. The manifesto published by Theo van Doesburg in 1924 can be read as a theoretical blueprint for the Schröder House.[8] At the same time, this leads to a one-sided and even erroneous approach to the design, especially when the term three-dimensional Mondrian is used. It is precisely in the use of color that Rietveld's approach is different, opposed even to that of Van Doesburg and Piet Mondrian.

In Rietveld's view the painter and architect handle color in fundamentally different ways, and they are therefore better off going their separate ways. After the Schröder House, that extreme color range had served its purpose for Rietveld. He went on to seek the reflection of light, which is the ultimate goal of color in architecture, in white, shades of gray and black. It is even possible that non-primary colors such as green, pink, orange and brown could be equally suitable for this purpose.

There are other aspects of Rietveld's architectural ideas, as seen in

リートフェルトは，画家と建築家の色彩の扱いには基本的な違いがあり，それぞれが自分たちの方法を用いるのが賢明であると考えていた。「シュレーダー邸」完成ののち，極端な色彩の使用はその目的を果たした。彼は，建築の色彩における究極の目的である光の反射を，白，灰色そして黒の濃淡に求めるようになった。緑，ピンク，オレンジ，茶といった補色もまた同様に，この目的にふさわしいものとなる。

「シュレーダー邸」には，リートフェルトの建築的アイディアを表すさらに重要な特性が備わっている。リートフェルトにとって，内部と外部の関係は常に建物の形態と配置に大きな影響を与えるものである。眺望は，彼の建築の最も美しい要素の一つである。彼はまた，廊下のような「無駄な」空間を避け，可能ならばホールを中心に部屋をまとめようとした。もう一つ，リートフェルトが生涯を通じ熱中したものは，1階平面を開放的に構成することであった。しかしながら，彼がこれを展開できたのは，「シュレーダー邸」といくつかの「空想に終わったデザイン」，そしてヴリーブルク・シネマの最上階にある自邸でのみである。

「シュレーダー邸」はリートフェルトの作品のみならず，近代建築全体の中でも，別格ともいうべき位置を占めている。それは実験であり，彼の「空間の視覚的なa-b-c」[9]の探求の一部であった。しかし，この小さな家の魅力的な美しさは，トゥルース・シュレーダーの新しい生活への憧れにも根ざしている。その本質は，建築は空間の創造であるというリートフェルトの信念を真に体現する並外れたデザインの多面的な特徴にあった。

参考文献：

テオドール・M・ブラウン『建築家G・リートフェルトの作品』[#1]（1958年，オランダ，ユトレヒト）；P・オーヴァリー他『リートフェルト・シュレーダー邸』[#2]（1988年，英国，ケンブリッジ）；奥佳弥『リートフェルトの建築』（2009年，日本，東京）；M・クーパー「ヘリット・リートフェルト」（1982年，英国，ロンドン／ケンブリッジ，C・ブロットカンプ編集『デ・ステイル：1917-1922形成期』）；M・クーパー，I・ファン・ゼイル『ヘリット・T・リートフェルト 1888-1964 作品集』（1992年，オランダ，ユトレヒト）；M・クーパー，W・クイスト，H・イベリング「ヘリット・T・リートフェルトの住宅」（2006年，『2G：インターナショナル・アーキテクチャ・レビュー』39/40合併号）；R・デッティングマイヤー，M・T・A・ファン・トール，I・ファン・ゼイル『リートフェルトの世界』（2010年，オランダ，ユトレヒト）；I・ファン・ゼイル『ヘリット・リートフェルト』[#3]（2010年，イギリス，ロンドン／ファイドン）

イダ・ファン・ゼイル博士は，ユトレヒト中央博物館，元キュレーター。

註：
1. https://whc.unesco.org/en/list/965
2. 参考文献#3, p.61
3. 参考文献#2, p.60
4. 参考文献#3, p.53
5. 参考文献#3, p.57
6. 1926年，G・リートフェルトがP・マースに宛てた手紙より（RSA0042 Rietveld Schröder Archive Utrecht）
7. 参考文献#2, pp.88-89
8. 参考文献#1, pp.65-69
9. 1958年，オランダ，ユトレヒトで行われた初の回顧展の中で，展示室の一つにつけられたタイトルより引用

the Schröder House, that are more significant and enduring. The relationship between interior and exterior always has a major influence on the form and situation of his houses. The view is often one of the most beautiful elements of the design. He also tries to avoid "useless" spaces like corridors, grouping the rooms around a hall, if possible. A second, life-long fascination of Rietveld was the open ground-plan, which, however, he was only able to develop in the Schröder House, in a few "fantasy designs," and in his own apartment on the top floor of the Vreeburg cinema.

The Schröder house has an exceptional position, not only in Rietveld's work but also in modern architecture as a whole. It was an experiment, part of his search for "a visual a-b-c- of space."[9] But the captivating beauty of this little house is also rooted in Truus Schröders' longing for a new life. Its intrinsic quality lies in the multi-faceted character of the extraordinary design that truly embodies Rietvelds' belief that architecture is the creation of space.

BIBLIOGRAPHY
Th. M. Brown, *The Work of G. Rietveld Architect*, Utrecht 1958 [#1]
P. Overy et.al., *The Rietveld Schröder House*, Cambridge 1988 [#2]
K. Oku, *The Architecture of Gerrit Th. Rietveld*, Tokyo 2009
M. Küper, 'Gerrit Rietveld,' in: C. Blotkamp (ed.), *De Stijl: the formative years, 1917-1922*, Cambridge/London 1982
M. Küper and I. van Zijl, *Gerrit Th. Rietveld 1888-1964. The Complete Works*, Utrecht 1992
M. Küper, W. Quist and H. Ibelings, 'Gerrit Th. Rietveld. Casas/Houses,' in *2G Revista internacinal de arquitectura/International Architectural Review*, 2006, no. 39/40
R. Dettingmijer, M. T. A. van Thoor, I. van Zijl, *Rietveld's Universe*, Rotterdam 2010
I. van Zijl, *Gerrit Rietveld*, Phaidon/London 2010 [#3]

Drs. Ida van Zijl worked as curator of Design and Applied Arts at the Centraal Museum Utrecht

NOTES:
1. https://whc.unesco.org/en/list/965
2. Bibl. #3, p. 61
3. Bibl. #2, p. 60
4. Bibl. #3, p.53
5. Bibl. #3, p. 57
6. Letter from G. Rietveld to P. Meurs, undated [1926] RSA0042 Rietveld Schröder Archive Utrecht
7. Bibl. #2, pp. 88-89
8. Bibl. #1, pp. 65-69
9. The title of the room of his first retrospective in Utrecht, 1958

Overall view from street

Street elevation on southwest

Southeast elevation on pedestrian walkway. House entrance on center

View from street corner

Entrance of studio on street

Bench at entrance of study

View from pedestrian walkway on east

Projected balcony and eaves.
Entrance on left

House entrance

Speaking tube for visitor and delivery receiving window

House entrance. Shelf with mail box

Entrance hall. Looking toward kitchen. Staircase to upper floor on left

Kitchen

Kitchen. Maid room is behind door. Service lift brings meals to upper floor

Corner of kitchen.
Wooden panel for shutter is set

Maid room. Dutch door to rear garden. Kitchen on right

Study on ground floor. Folding table and built-in furniture

Studio on ground floor facing street. Rietveld used as work space until 1933

Staircase to upper living space. Closable yellow sliding door

Spiral staircases

Living space with movable partitions open

Living space with movable partitions open. Red-floor space for son

Living space with movable partitions open.
Daughters' room on left, Truus Schröder's bedroom on right immost

Living space with movable partitions open. Looking from dining room.
Record player and projector are set in yellow built-in furniture

Son's room. View toward balcony facing pedestrian walkway

Daughters' room. View toward balcony facing street

Son's room with partitions

Daughters' room with partitions

Dining room with partitions

View toward daughters' room with partitions, door opened

Staircase with ladder to roof, glass walls and handrail panels covered

Staircase with ladder to roof, glass walls and handrail panels covered

Truus Schröder's bedroom. Bathroom on left

Washbasin at Truus Schröder's bedroom

Bathroom

Dining room

Dining room. Truus Schröder's bedroom behind cupboard. Service lift on right

Windows of dining room opened toward outside

Dining room with windows open

Interior photographs: © PICTORIGHT, Amsterdam & JASPAR, Tokyo, 2021 E4492
pp.12-13:
no.004 A 072
Gerrit Thomas Rietveld (1888-Utrecht 1964)
Rietveld Schröder House (Schröder-Schräder residence) ca. 1950-1950 for De Stijl tent. 1951
Lichtdruk van 004 A 059, voordat deze is verduidelijkt met de contouren van de daklijn en de stoppen vergroot zijn van stippen tot cirkeltjes.
Ingekleurd met witte, blauwe, rode, grijze, zwarte en gele verf en geplakt op grijs karton
Rietveld Schröder Archive / Central Museum, Utrecht
© Central Museum Utrecht / PICTORIGHT

Photographs are taken by Yoshio Futagawa except as noted below.
pp.22-23, pp.26-27, p.28, p.30 right, pp.44-45: photos by Yukio Futagawa

'The Rietveld Schröder House' by Ida van Zijl has revised for this issue from "GA 68 The Schröder House" (A.D.A. EDITA Tokyo, 1992)

イダ・ファン・ゼイルによるエッセイ「リートフェルト・シュレーダー邸」は，『GA 68 ヘリット・トーマス・リートフェルト シュローダー邸』（エーディーエー・エディタ・トーキョー発行，1992年）より本書の為に加筆，改訂された。

世界現代住宅全集 32
ヘリット・リートフェルト
リートフェルト・シュレーダー邸
2021年12月24日発行
文：イダ・ファン・ゼイル
撮影・編集：二川由夫
アート・ディレクション：細谷巖

印刷・製本：大日本印刷株式会社
制作・発行：エーディーエー・エディタ・トーキョー
151-0051　東京都渋谷区千駄ヶ谷 3-12-14
TEL.（03）3403-1581（代）

禁無断転載

ISBN 978-4-87140-565-2 C1352